W9-BLQ-278

ESSENTIAL ELEMENTS 2000

COMPREHENSIVE BAND METHOD

TIM LAUTZENHEISER
PAUL LAVENDER

JOHN HIGGINS
TOM C. RHODES

CHARLES MENGHINI
DON BIERSCHENK

CONGRATULATIONS and welcome to **Essential Elements 2000 – Book 2!**

PLAY ALONG CD DISC 1

Your book includes the **Play Along CD Disc 1** which covers two different sections of Book 2:

- The first 55 exercises —*and*—
- The Individual Study section (pages 38–41)

During the first 55 exercises, the melody is demonstrated by a small band ensemble. A professional soloist is featured **playing your instrument** for the Individual Study section.

Each track begins with a one measure count-off, and it is played **twice**—the second time is the accompaniment-only. These track accompaniments are performed by professional studio musicians, and they explore a rich variety of musical styles and cultures, with classical, rock, jazz, country, and world music.

PLAY ALONG CD SET – DISC 2 & 3

This set of play-along tracks is available from your music dealer, and includes exercise 56 through the end of Book 2. It features the melody demonstrated by a small band ensemble, followed by the accompaniment-only. For use by all instruments.

ISBN 0-634-01297-5

HAL•LEONARD® CORPORATION

7777 W. BLUEMOUND RD. P.O. BOX 13819 MILWAUKEE, WI 53213

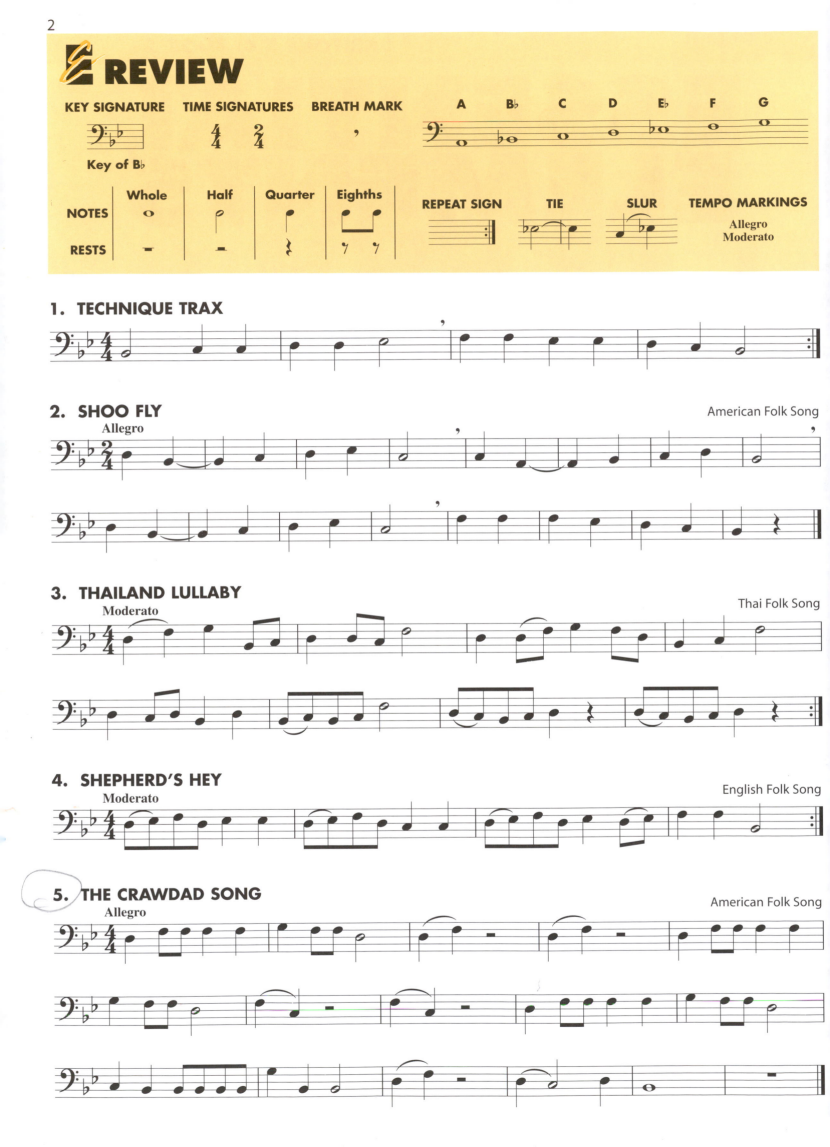

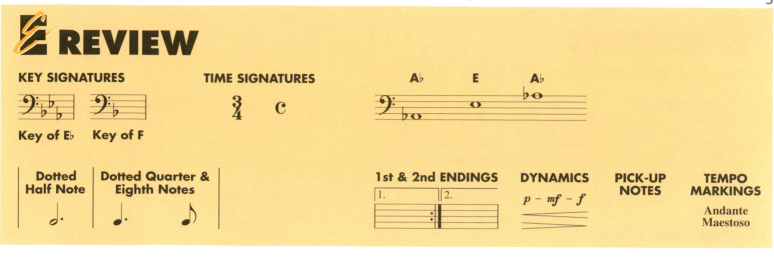

REVIEW

KEY SIGNATURES

Key of E♭ Key of F

TIME SIGNATURES

3/4 C

A♭ E A♭

Dotted Half Note

Dotted Quarter & Eighth Notes

1st & 2nd ENDINGS

DYNAMICS

p – mf – f

PICK-UP NOTES

TEMPO MARKINGS

Andante
Maestoso

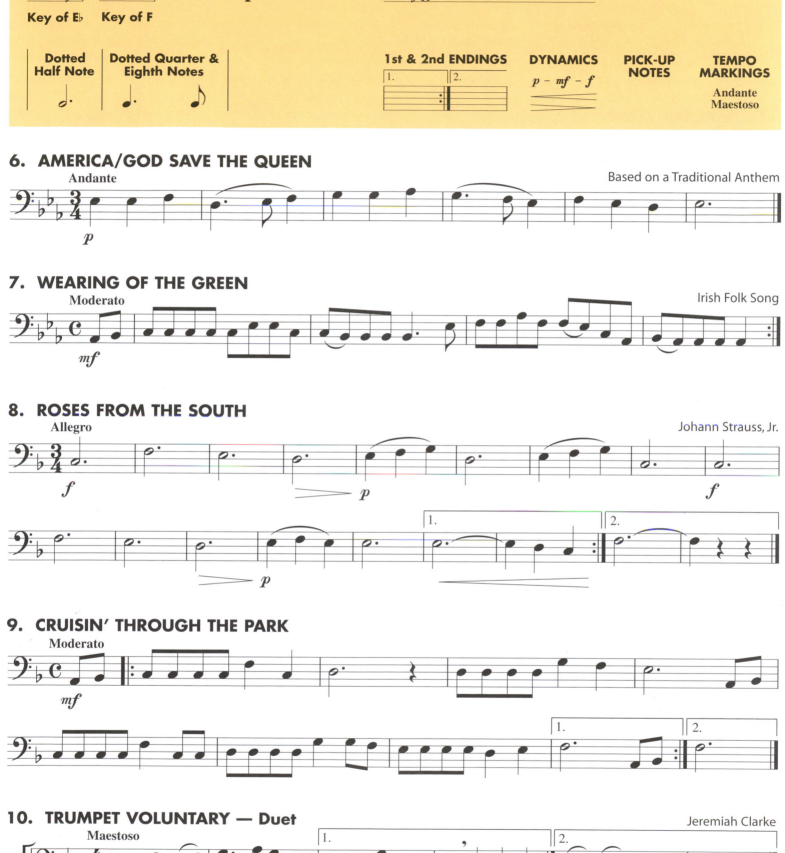

6. AMERICA/GOD SAVE THE QUEEN

Andante

Based on a Traditional Anthem

7. WEARING OF THE GREEN

Moderato

Irish Folk Song

8. ROSES FROM THE SOUTH

Allegro

Johann Strauss, Jr.

9. CRUISIN' THROUGH THE PARK

Moderato

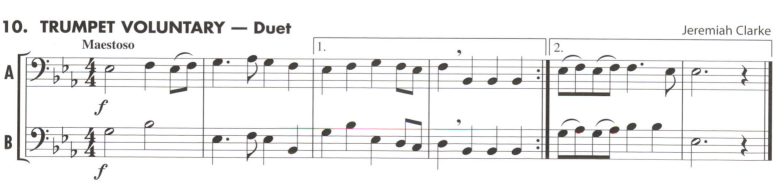

10. TRUMPET VOLUNTARY — Duet

Maestoso

Jeremiah Clarke

A

B

4

 **REVIEW**

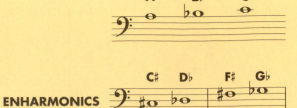

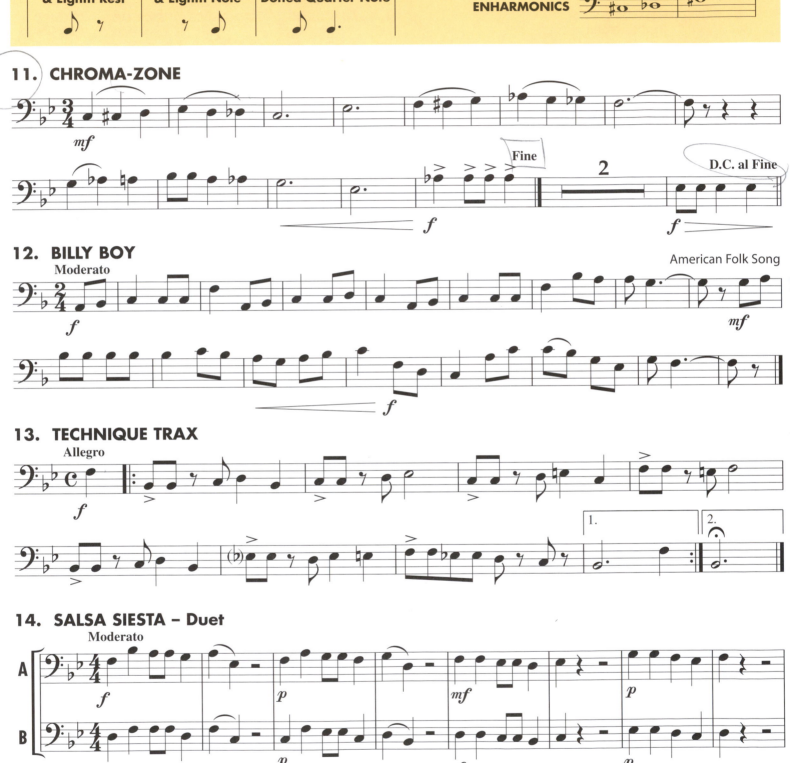

Staccato

Staccato notes are played lightly and with separation. They are marked with a dot above or below the note.

15. TREADING LIGHTLY

Moderato

Tenuto

Tenuto notes are played smoothly and connected, holding each note until the next is played. They are marked with a straight line above or below the note.

16. SMOOTH MOVE

Moderato

17. SHIFTING GEARS

Moderato

18. TALLIS CANON (Round)

Moderato

Thomas Tallis

Sightreading

Sightreading means playing a musical piece for the first time. The key to sightreading success is to know what to look for *before* you play. Use the word **S-T-A-R-S** to remind yourself what to look for, and eventually your band will become sightreading STARS!

S — **Sharps or flats** in the key signature
T — **Time signature** and **tempo markings**
A — **Accidentals** not found in the key signature
R — **Rhythms**, silently counting the more difficult notes and rests
S — **Signs**, including dynamics, articulations, repeats and endings

19. SIGHTREADING CHALLENGE

Moderato

DAILY WARM-UPS

WORK-OUTS FOR TONE & TECHNIQUE

20. TONE BUILDER

21. FLEXIBILITY STUDY

22. TECHNIQUE TRAX

23. CHORALE

Johann Sebastian Bach

Andante

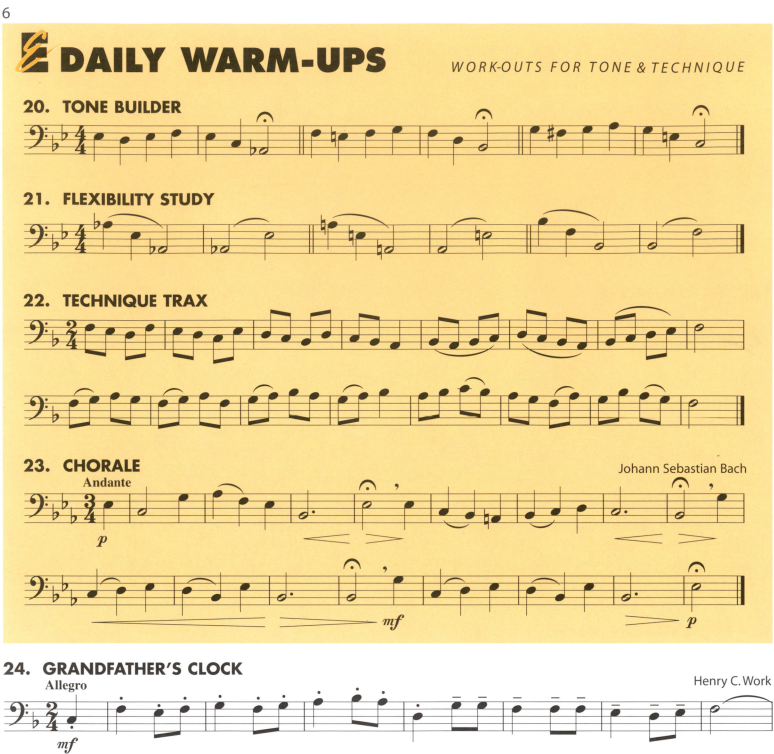

24. GRANDFATHER'S CLOCK

Henry C. Work

Allegro

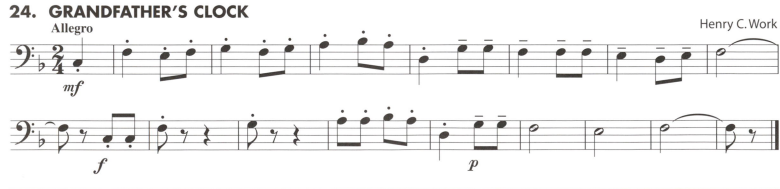

Ritardando   *ritard.* (or) *rit.* – Gradually slower

25. GLOW WORM

Paul Lincke

Allegretto ◄ *Usually a little slower than Allegro, and with a lighter style.*

rit. ◄ Watch your director.

26. ALMA MATER – New Note *Practice long tones on all new notes.*

A.C. Weekes, W.M. Smith, H.S. Thompson

HISTORY

The Scottish folk song *Loch Lomond* is credited to an anonymous soldier who was imprisoned and awaiting execution. In it he writes of his desire to return home to his family and the breathtaking beauty of Loch (Lake) Lomond, a lake in Scotland. Located in the southern highlands, the lake is almost entirely surrounded by hills. One of these is Ben Lomond, a peak 3,192 feet high.

27. LOCH LOMOND

Scottish Folk Song

Key Changes

THEORY

If a key signature changes during a piece of music, you will usually see a thin double bar line at the **key change**. You may also see natural signs reminding you to "cancel" previous sharps or flats. Keep playing, using the correct notes indicated in the *new* key signature.

28. MOLLY MALONE

Irish Folk Song

Dynamics

cresc. = crescendo (or) ———
decresc. = decrescendo (or) ———

29. RISE AND FALL

30. NO COMPARISON

31. SIGHTREADING CHALLENGE *Remember the S-T-A-R-S guidelines.*

 **THEORY**

¢ Time Signature
Cut Time (Alla Breve)

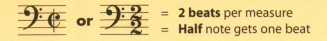 or = **2 beats** per measure
= **Half** note gets one beat

𝅝 = 2 beats
𝅗𝅥 = 1 beat
♩ = ½ beat

32. RHYTHM RAP *Clap the rhythm while counting and tapping.*

1 & 2 & 1 & 2 & 1 & 2 & 1 & 2 & 1 & 2 & 1 & 2 & 1 & 2 & 1 & 2 & 1 & 2 &

33. A CUT ABOVE

1 & 2 & 1 & 2 & 1 & 2 & 1 & 2 & 1 & 2 & 1 & 2 & 1 & 2 & 1 & 2 &

34. TWO-FOUR YANKEE DOODLE

American Folk Song

35. CUT TIME YANKEE DOODLE

American Folk Song

36. MARIANNE

Jamaican Folk Song

37. THE VICTORS

Louis Elbel

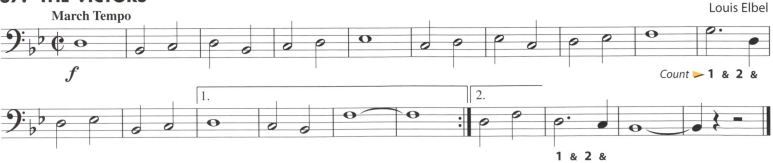

38. ESSENTIAL CREATIVITY *Write this example in cut time ¢ before playing.*

Dynamics

mp — *mezzo piano* (moderately soft)

Use full breath support at all dynamic levels.

p — *mp* — *mf* — *f*

39. A - ROVING

Moderato

mp · *f* · *mp*

Syncopation

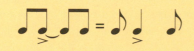

THEORY

Syncopation occurs when an accent or emphasis is given to a note that is not on a strong beat. This type of "off-beat" feel is common in many popular and classical styles.

40. RHYTHM RAP

1 & 2 & 1 & 2 & 1 & 2 & 1 & 2 & 1 & 2 & 1 & 2 & 1 & 2 & 1 & 2 & 1 & 2 &

41. IN SYNC

1 & 2 & 1 & 2 & 1 & 2 & 1 & 2 & 1 & 2 & 1 & 2 & 1 & 2 & 1 & 2 &

42. LA ROCA

Moderato

Puerto Rican Folk Song

f · *mp* · *f* · *f*

HISTORY

43. ESSENTIAL ELEMENTS QUIZ – YOU'RE A GRAND OLD FLAG

March Style

Words and Music by George M. Cohan

mf · *mp* · *cresc.* · *f* · *cresc.* · *mp* · *cresc.* · *f*

THEORY

New Key Signature

This key signature indicates your **Key of C** (no sharps or flats).

44. KEY MOMENT – New Note

B

C Scale ▼ B *Arpeggio*

45. THE MINSTREL BOY

Irish Folk Song

Andante

mp 1. , 2.

46. CLOSE CALL – New Note

B

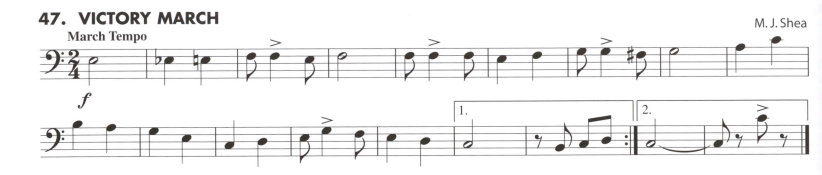

▲ B 1. 2.

47. VICTORY MARCH

M. J. Shea

March Tempo

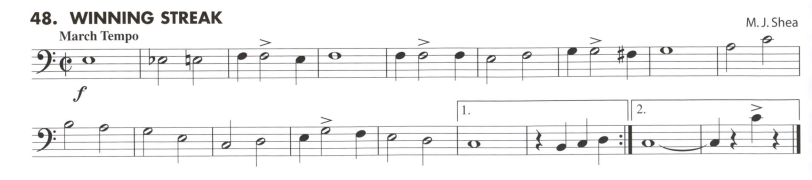

f 1. 2.

THEORY

Cut Time Syncopation

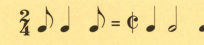

Compare the notation of the melody below with *Victory March* above. Should they sound the same?

48. WINNING STREAK

M. J. Shea

March Tempo

f 1. 2.

49. SIGHTREADING CHALLENGE *Remember the S-T-A-R-S guidelines.*

Moderato

mp *mf* *mp*

Sixteenth Notes

4 sixteenth notes = 1 Beat
Each sixteenth note = ¼ Beat

A single sixteenth note has 2 flags on the stem.

50. RHYTHM RAP

51. SIXTEENTH NOTE FANFARE

52. MOVING ALONG

53. BACK AND FORTH – Duet

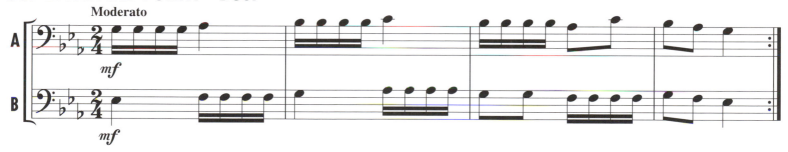

54. COMIN' ROUND THE MOUNTAIN VARIATIONS

American Folk Song

55. ESSENTIAL ELEMENTS QUIZ

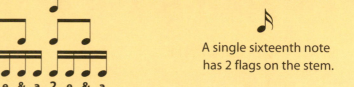

PE FO MANCE S TLIGHT

56. WARM-UP CHORALE

J. S. Bach/Arr. by John Higgins

57. THE THUNDERER – Band Arrangement

John Philip Sousa
Arr. by John Higgins

Reproduced by Permission of Boosey & Hawkes Music Publishers Ltd.

58. HILL AND GULLY RIDER – Band Arrangement

Jamaican Folk Song
Arr. by John Higgins

59. SHENANDOAH – Band Arrangement

American Folk Song
Arr. by John Higgins

PERFORMANCE SPOTLIGHT

60. LAS MAÑANITAS – Band Arrangement

Mexican Folk Song
Arr. by John Higgins

61. RONDEAU – Band Arrangement

Jean-Joseph Mouret
Arr. by John Higgins

D.S. al Fine–Go back to the sign (𝄋) and play until **Fine**.

62. ROCK.COM – Encore Band Arrangement

John Higgins

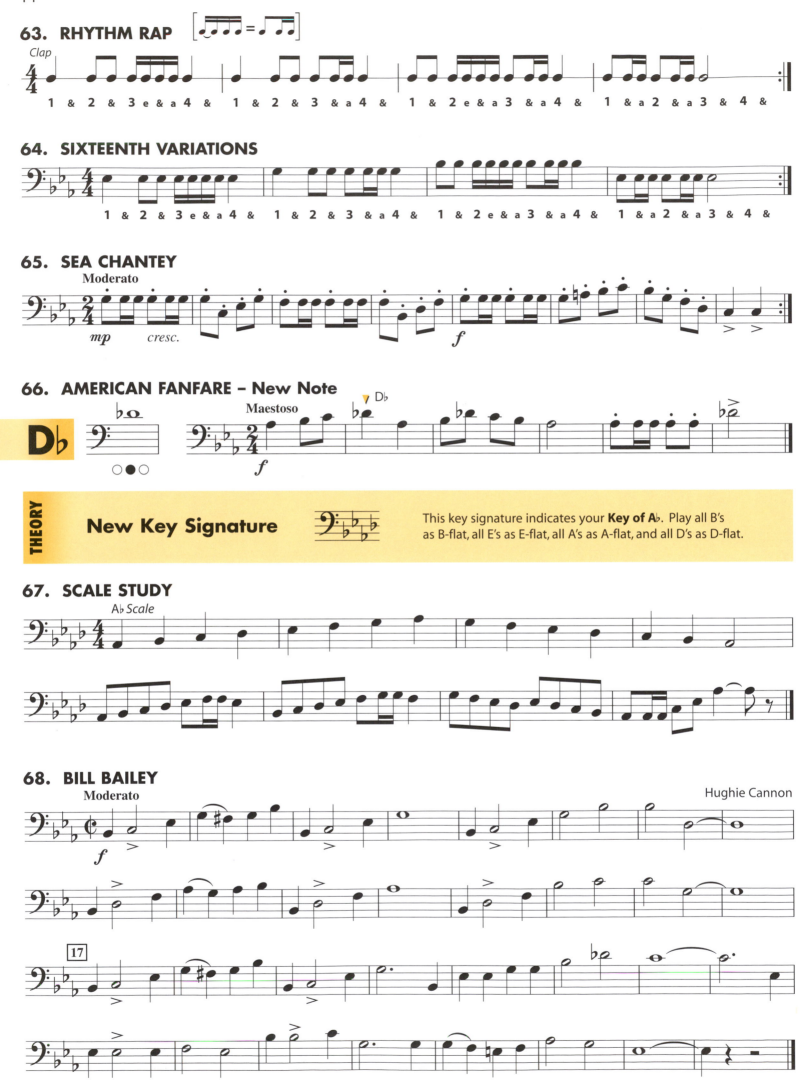

63. RHYTHM RAP

64. SIXTEENTH VARIATIONS

65. SEA CHANTEY

66. AMERICAN FANFARE – New Note

Db

THEORY

New Key Signature

This key signature indicates your **Key of Ab.** Play all B's as B-flat, all E's as E-flat, all A's as A-flat, and all D's as D-flat.

67. SCALE STUDY

Ab Scale

68. BILL BAILEY

Hughie Cannon

Moderato

Rallentando   *rall.*   –   Gradually slower (same as ritardando)

75. SIMPLE SONG – Duet

76. LINE DANCE

77. TECHNIQUE TRAX

▲ *Keep 16ths steady*

78. THE GALWAY PIPER

Irish Reel

79. MANHATTAN BEACH MARCH

John Philip Sousa

80. SIGHTREADING CHALLENGE *Remember the S-T-A-R-S guidelines.*

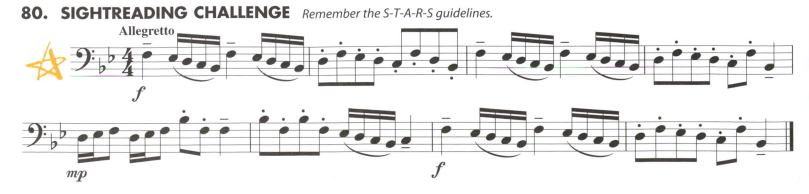

DAILY WARM-UPS

WORK-OUTS FOR TONE & TECHNIQUE

87. TONE BUILDER *Play at a very slow tempo.*

88. FLEXIBILITY STUDY

89. TECHNIQUE TRAX

90. CHORALE

Johann Sebastian Bach

HISTORY French composer **Georges Bizet** (1838–1875) entered the Paris Conservatory to study music when he was only ten years old. There he won many awards for voice, piano, organ, and composition. Bizet's best known composition is the opera *Carmen,* which was first performed in 1875. *Carmen* tells the story of a band of Gypsies, soldiers, smugglers, and outlaws. Originally criticized for its realism on stage, it was soon hailed as the most popular French opera ever written.

91. TOREADOR SONG (from CARMEN)

Georges Bizet

92. LA CUMPARSITA

G. Rodriguez

Enharmonics

93. THE YELLOW ROSE OF TEXAS *Check the key signature.*

American Folk Song

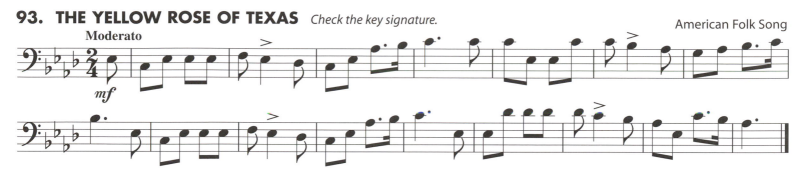

94. SCALE STUDY – New Note

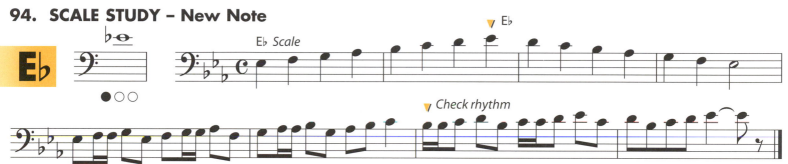

Until 1974 Australia's official national anthem was *God Save The Queen*. A competition was held in 1973 to compose a new anthem, but none of the entries met with the judges' approval. Finally the government asked the public to vote, choosing from among Australia's 3 most popular patriotic songs. After easily defeating *Waltzing Matilda* and *God Save The Queen*, *Advance Australia Fair* was officially declared the national anthem of Australia on April 19, 1974.

95. ADVANCE AUSTRALIA FAIR

Peter Dodds McCormick

rit.   *a tempo*
△ Resume previous tempo

96. ESSENTIAL CREATIVITY

Arrange the melody of "America (My Country 'Tis Of Thee)" for your instrument. Write out the first line (6 measures).
Your first note is F. ADD: Key signature—key of F • Time signature—3/4 • Tempo and dynamic markings.

Play the completed line on your instrument to hear your own version.

97. AMERICAN PATROL

F. W. Meacham

Moderato

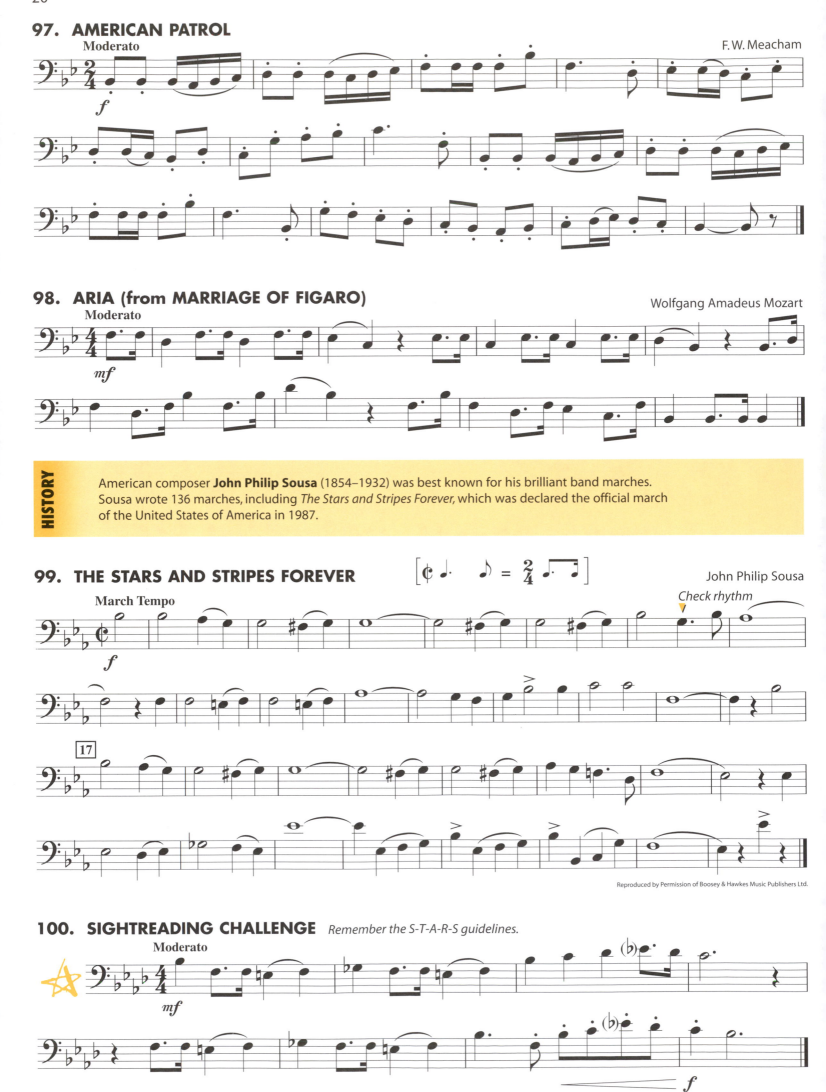

98. ARIA (from MARRIAGE OF FIGARO)

Wolfgang Amadeus Mozart

Moderato

99. THE STARS AND STRIPES FOREVER

John Philip Sousa

March Tempo

Check rhythm

17

Reproduced by Permission of Boosey & Hawkes Music Publishers Ltd.

100. SIGHTREADING CHALLENGE *Remember the S-T-A-R-S guidelines.*

Moderato

6/8 Time Signature

$\mathbf{9}{:}\,\dfrac{6}{8}$ = **6 beats** per measure
= **Eighth** note gets one beat

♪ = 1 beat   ♩ = 2 beats
♩. = 3 beats   ♩♪ = 6 beats

THEORY

6/8 time is usually played with a slight emphasis on the **1st** and **4th** beats of each measure. This divides the measure into 2 groups of 3 beats each. In faster music, these two primary beats will make the music feel like it's counted "in 2."

101. RHYTHM RAP   *Clap the rhythm while counting and tapping.*

102. LAZY DAY

103. ROW YOUR BOAT

104. JOLLY GOOD FELLOW

105. CHANSON

106. ESSENTIAL ELEMENTS QUIZ – WHEN JOHNNY COMES MARCHING HOME

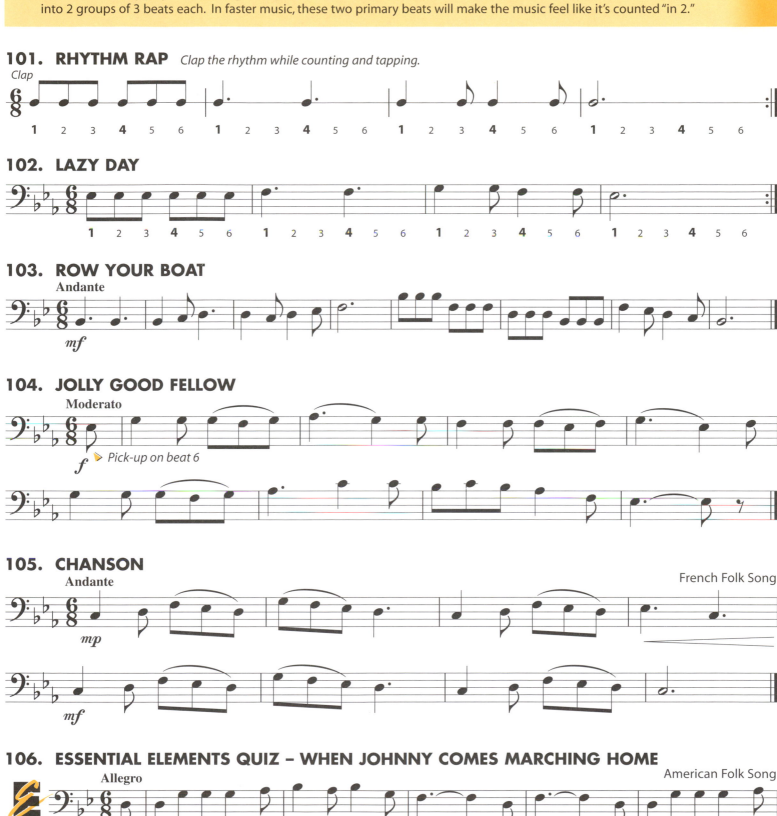
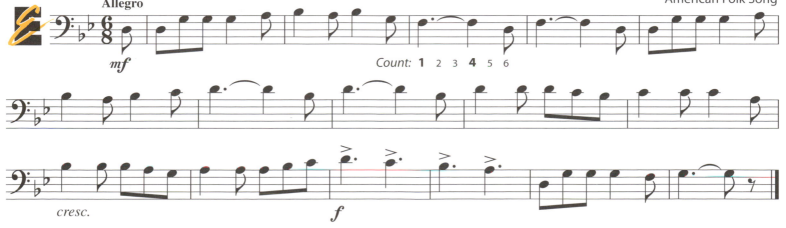

THEORY

More Enharmonics

Remember that notes which sound the same but have different letter names are called **enharmonics.** These are some common enharmonics that you'll use in the exercises below.

More Chromatics

The smallest distance between two notes is a half-step, and a scale made up of consecutive half-steps is a **chromatic scale.** These are usually written with **enharmonic** notes—sharps when going up and flats when going down.

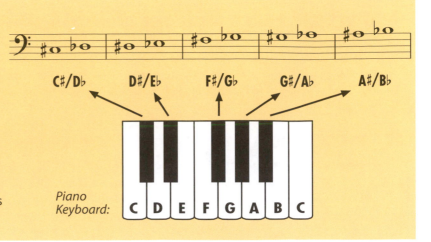

Piano Keyboard:

---

107. CHROMATIC SCALE

Practice slowly until you are sure of all the fingerings.

△ E♭ Enharmonic   △ A♭ Enharmonic

---

108. TECHNIQUE TRAX

HISTORY

A **Habañera** is a Cuban dance and song form in slow 2/4 meter. It is named after the city of Havana, the capital of Cuba. Made popular in the New World in the early 19th Century, it was later carried over to Spain. There the rhythms of the Habañera were incorporated into many styles of Latin music. One of the most famous Habañeras is heard in Bizet's *Carmen,* written in 1875.

---

109. HABAÑERA (from CARMEN)

Andante   Georges Bizet

---

110. CHROMATIC CRESCENDO

Moderato

111. TURKISH MARCH (from THE RUINS OF ATHENS)

Ludwig van Beethoven

112. THE OVERLANDER

Australian Folk Song

113. STACCATO STUDY

114. YANKEE DOODLE DANDY

Words and Music by George M. Cohan

115. SIGHTREADING CHALLENGE

Remember the **S-T-A-R-S** guidelines:
S – Sharps or flats in the key signature, **T** – Time signature and tempos, **A** – Accidentals, **R** – Rhythm, **S** – Signs

Triplets

A **triplet** is a group of **3** notes played in the space of **2**. In $\frac{2}{4}$, $\frac{3}{4}$, or $\frac{4}{4}$ time, an eighth note triplet is spread evenly across one beat.

116. RHYTHM RAP

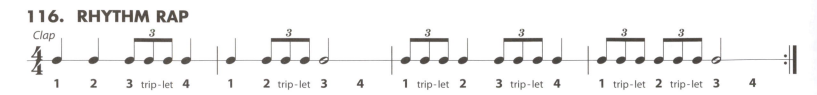

117. THREE TO GET READY

118. TRIPLET STUDY

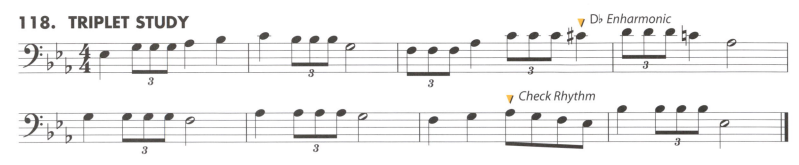

119. MARCH (from THE NUTCRACKER) – Duet

Peter I. Tchaikovsky

120. ESSENTIAL ELEMENTS QUIZ – THEME FROM FAUST

Charles Gounod

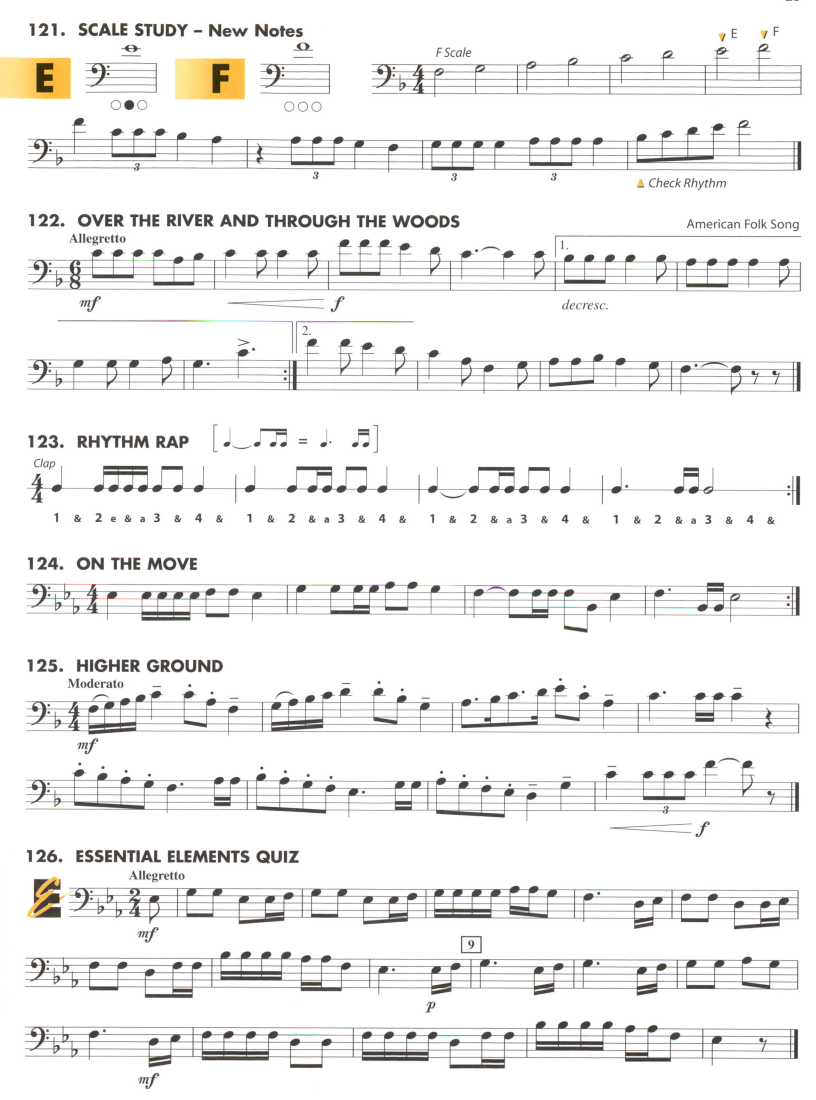

The first known printing of the lyrics and music to **The Marines' Hymn** dates from August 1, 1918. An unknown author is believed to have taken the opening words of the song from the words on the Marine Corps flag, "From the halls of Montezuma to the shores of Tripoli." The music was taken from "Genevieve de Brabant," by the operetta composer Jacques Offenbach.

127. THE MARINES' HYMN

D.S. al Fine

Play until you see the **D.S. al Fine**. Then go back to the sign (𝄋) and play until the word **Fine**. **D.S.** is the abbreviation for **Dal Segno**, or "from the sign," and **Fine** means "the end."

128. D.S. MARCH

Accelerando

accel. – Gradually faster.

129. CAN–CAN

Jacques Offenbach

▲ *Watch your director.*

130. TARANTELLA

Allegro

Italian Folk Song

f　Pick-up　　　　　　　　　　　　　　　　　　　mf

131. EMPEROR WALTZ

Andantino ◁ *Tempo between Andante and Moderato.*

Johann Strauss, Jr.

Legato Style

legato – Played in a smooth, connected style.

132. ENGLISH DANCE – Duet

Andante

Johann Christian Bach

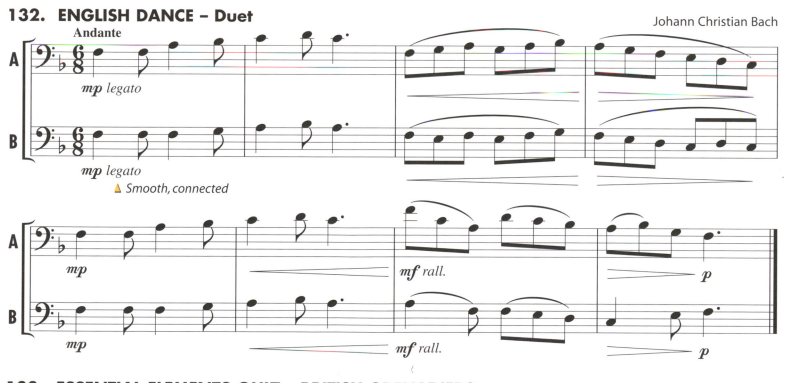

△ Smooth, connected

133. ESSENTIAL ELEMENTS QUIZ – BRITISH GRENADIERS

Allegretto

Traditional

134. NASSAU BOUND

Bahamian Folk Song

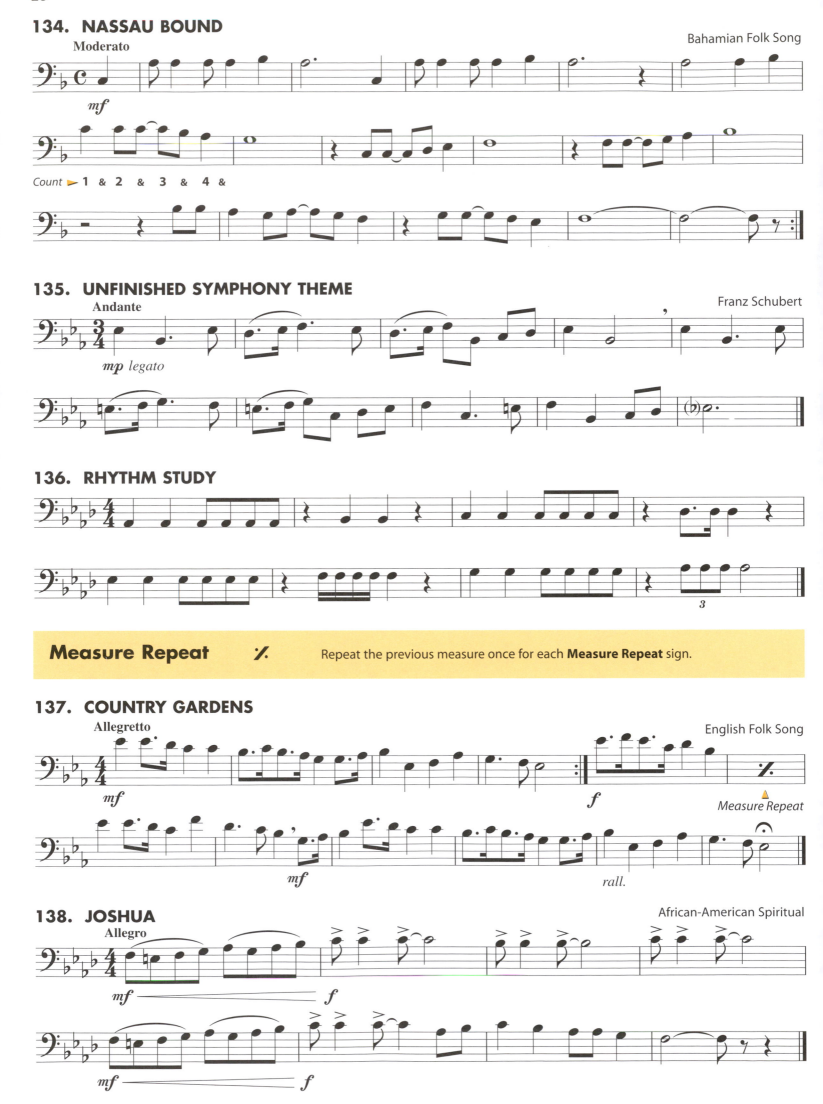

Count ▶ **1 & 2 & 3 & 4 &**

135. UNFINISHED SYMPHONY THEME

Franz Schubert

136. RHYTHM STUDY

Measure Repeat   ⅍   Repeat the previous measure once for each **Measure Repeat** sign.

137. COUNTRY GARDENS

English Folk Song

Measure Repeat

rall.

138. JOSHUA

African-American Spiritual

139. LISTEN TO THE MOCKINGBIRD

Alice Hawthorne

140. ANCHORS AWEIGH

Capt. A.H. Miles and C.A. Zimmerman

141. GREENSLEEVES

English Folk Song

142. THE LONG CLIMB

▲ Measure Repeat

143. THE BLUE BELLS OF SCOTLAND

Scottish Folk Song

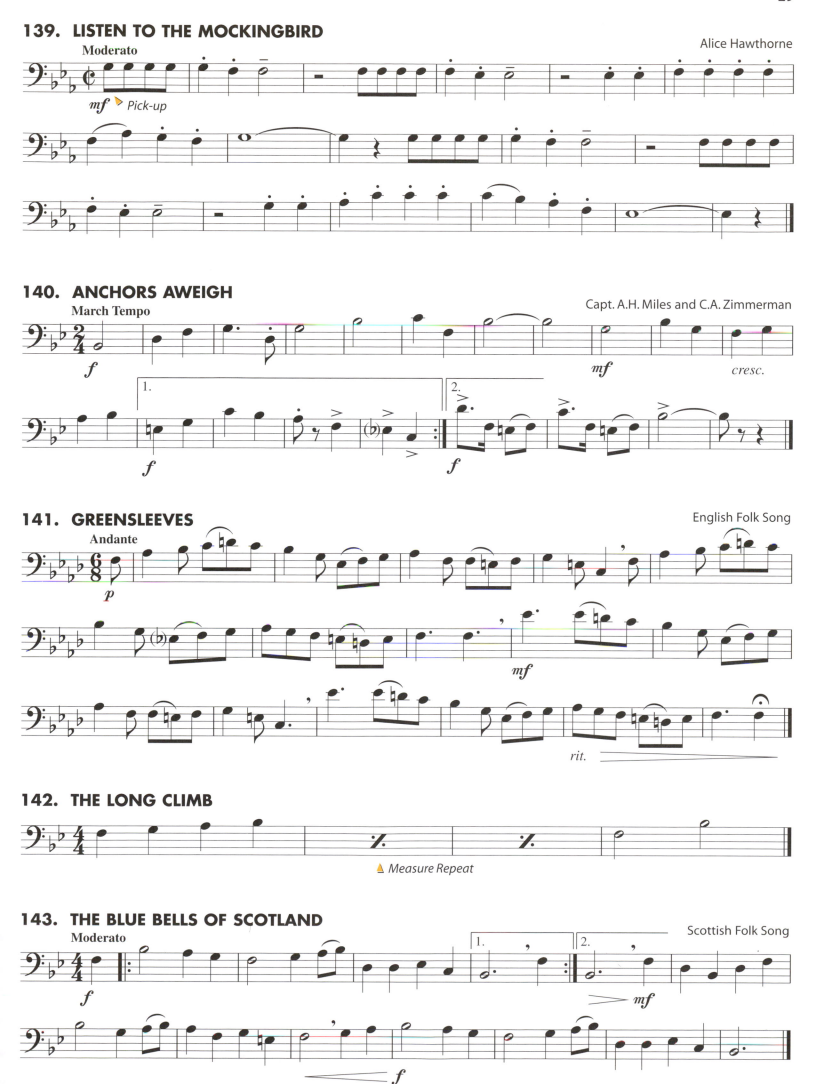

Major and Minor

The scales you've already learned are called **Major** scales. They all follow the same pattern, with **half-steps** between notes 3–4 and between notes 7–8.

Natural Minor scales follow a different pattern, with **half-steps** between notes 2–3 and 5–6. The **G Minor** scale uses the same key signature as **B♭ Major**.

Another type of minor scale is called **Harmonic Minor**, which adds an accidental to raise the **7th** note by a half-step. Compare the scales on the right.

See page 37 for additional minor scales.

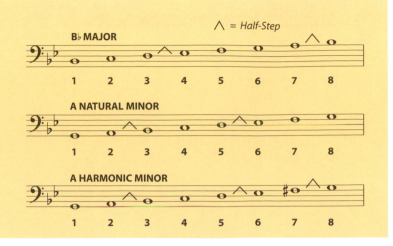

144. NATURAL MINOR SCALE – New Note

145. FINALE FROM "NEW WORLD SYMPHONY"

Antonin Dvořák

146. HARMONIC MINOR SCALE

147. HUNGARIAN DANCE NO. 5

Johannes Brahms

148. POMP AND CIRCUMSTANCE (LAND OF HOPE AND GLORY)

Edward Elgar

PE FORMANCE SPOTLIGHT

149. SIMPLE GIFTS – Band Arrangement

Shaker Folk Song
Arr. by John Higgins

150. SEMPER FIDELIS – Band Arrangement

John Philip Sousa
Arr. by John Higgins

PERFORMANCE SPOTLIGHT

151. DANNY BOY – Band Arrangement

Irish Folk Song
Arr. by John Higgins

152. TAKE ME OUT TO THE BALL GAME – Band Arrangement

By Jack Norworth and Harry von Tilzer
Arr. by John Higgins

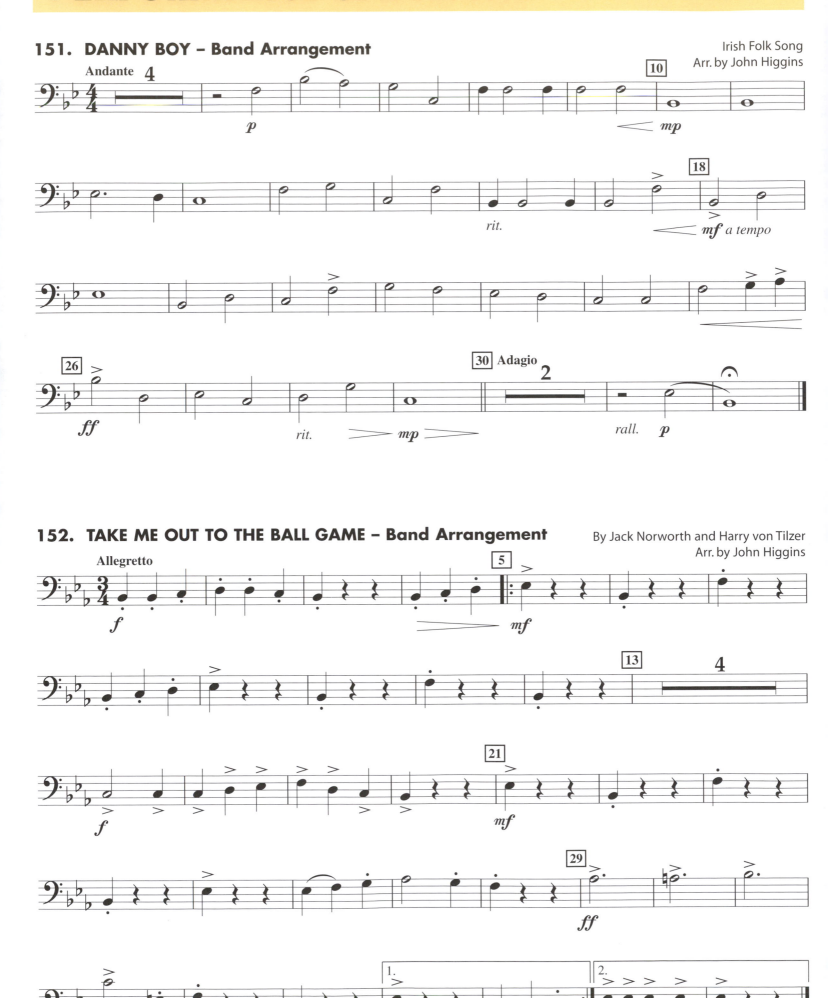

PERFORMANCE SPOTLIGHT

153. SERENGETI (AFRICAN RHAPSODY) – Band Arrangement

John Higgins

RUBANK® STUDIES

154. CHORALE

155. CHORALE

156. CHORALE

157. CHORALE

158. CHORALE

KEY OF B♭

159.

160.

161.

162.

35

RUBANK® STUDIES

KEY OF E♭

KEY OF F

RUBANK® STUDIES

KEY OF A♭

RUBANK® STUDIES

KEY OF G MINOR

INDIVIDUAL STUDY – Baritone B.C.

187. LOW NOTE EXCURSION – New Note   *CD Track 56*

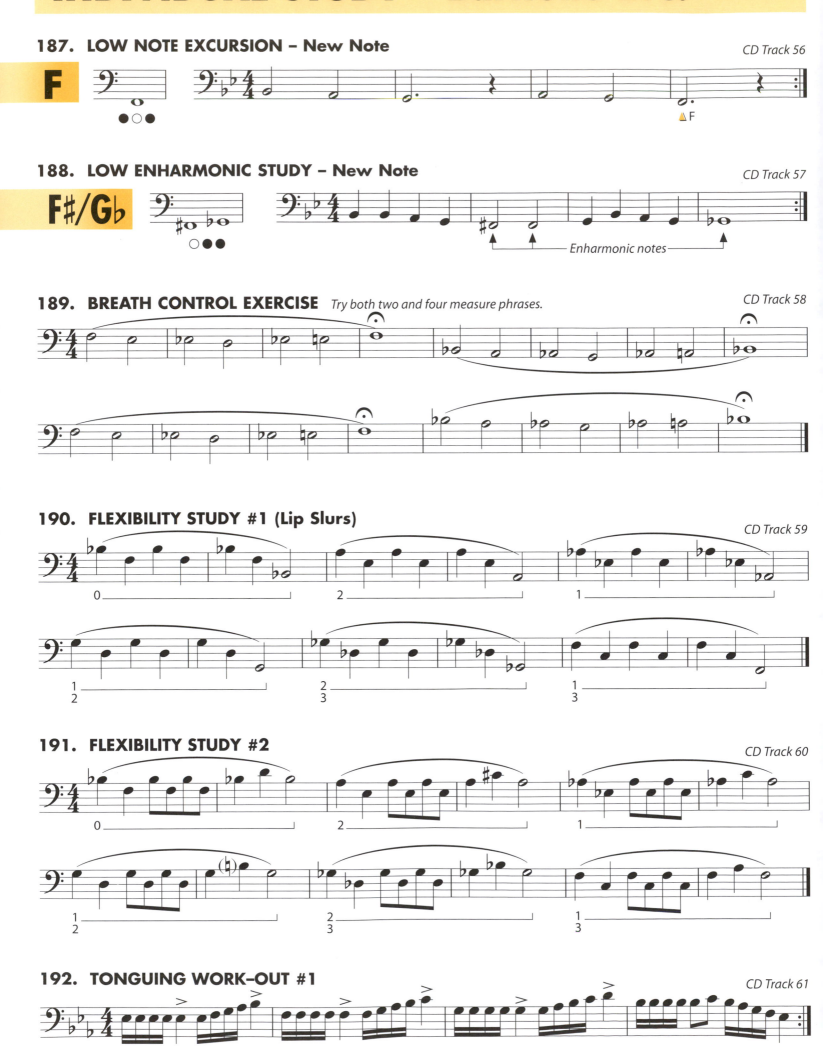

188. LOW ENHARMONIC STUDY – New Note   *CD Track 57*

Enharmonic notes

189. BREATH CONTROL EXERCISE *Try both two and four measure phrases.*   *CD Track 58*

190. FLEXIBILITY STUDY #1 (Lip Slurs)   *CD Track 59*

191. FLEXIBILITY STUDY #2   *CD Track 60*

192. TONGUING WORK-OUT #1   *CD Track 61*

INDIVIDUAL STUDY – Baritone B.C.

193. TONGUING WORK-OUT #2
CD Track 62

194. FINGER PATTERNS
CD Track 63

195. ARTICULATION STUDY #1
CD Track 64

196. ARTICULATION STUDY #2
CD Track 65

197. ARTICULATION STUDY #3
CD Track 66

198. CHROMATIC CHALLENGE
CD Track 67

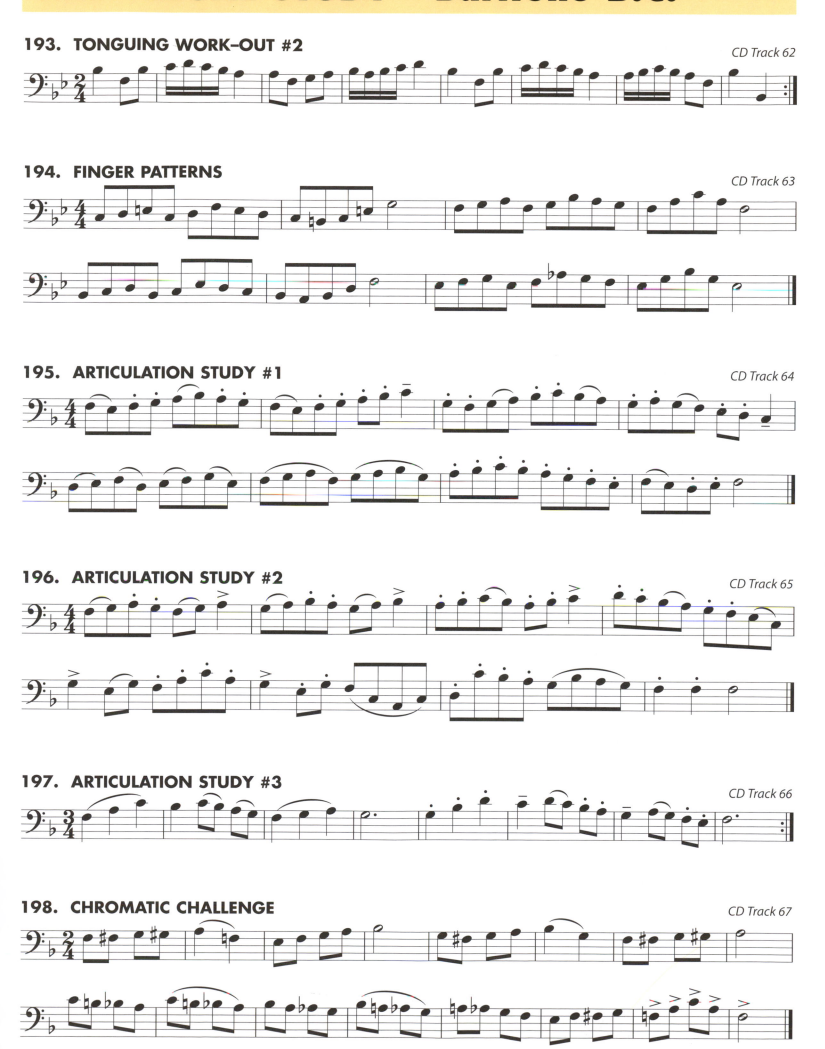

INDIVIDUAL STUDY – Baritone B.C.

Solo with Piano Accompaniment

You can perform this solo with the piano accompaniment on the following page.

199. GARNET – Baritone B.C. Solo *CD Track 68*

Vander Cook

INDIVIDUAL STUDY – Baritone B.C.

199. GARNET – Piano Accompaniment *CD Track 69*

Vander Cook

RHYTHM STUDIES

RHYTHM STUDIES

CREATING MUSIC

THEORY

Theme and Variation

Theme and Variation is a technique used by composers and arrangers to create interesting musical ideas that are "varied" from an established melody, or "theme." Play the following theme and two variations to hear how the arranger has created new phrases based on the original melody.

1. THEME

"Simple Gifts"

VARIATION 1 *Adding some notes • Changing some rhythms*

VARIATION 2 *Removing notes • Changing rhythms • Adding accents • Adding notes*

2. THEME AND YOUR VARIATION *Write your own variation of this theme. Use your instrument to hear and try different ideas.*

Theme

"Oh, Susanna"

Your Variation

THEORY

Blues Improvisation

Improvisation using a **Blues Scale** is an important part of jazz and popular music. Musicians use combinations of these notes and various rhythms to create their own spontaneous solos over a 12 measure progression of chords.

Blues Scale

3. LET'S JAM *Use the indicated notes from the Blues Scale to create your own solo to play with the accompaniment (Line B).*

You can mark your progress through the book on this page. Fill in the stars as instructed by your band director.

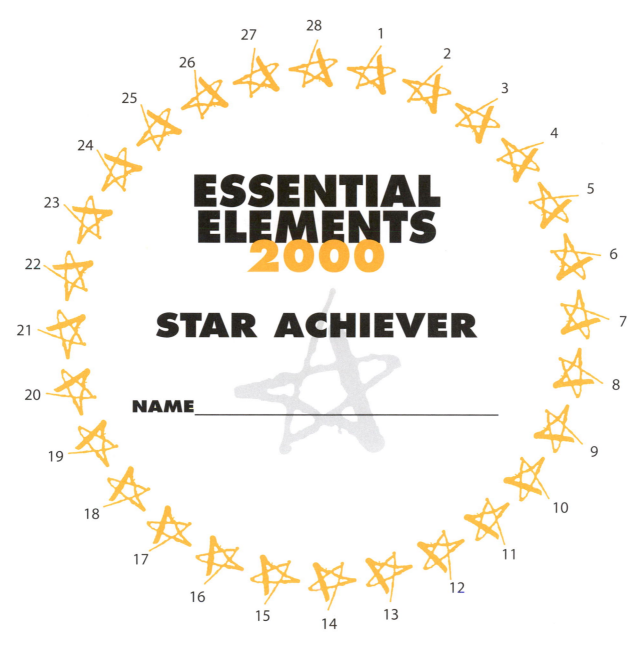

ESSENTIAL
ELEMENTS
2000

STAR ACHIEVER

NAME_____

1. Page 2–4, Review
2. Page 5, Sightreading Challenge, No. 19
3. Page 6, Daily Warm-Ups
4. Page 7, Sightreading Challenge, No. 31
5. Page 8, Essential Creativity, No. 38
6. Page 9, EE Quiz, No. 43
7. Page 10, Sightreading Challenge, No. 49
8. Page 11, EE Quiz, No. 55
9. Page 12–13, Performance Spotlight
10. Page 15, EE Quiz, No. 74
11. Page 16, Sightreading Challenge, No. 80
12. Page 18, Daily Warm-Ups
13. Page 19, Essential Creativity, No. 96
14. Page 20, Sightreading Challenge, No. 100
15. Page 21, EE Quiz, No. 106
16. Page 22, Chromatic Scale, No. 107
17. Page 23, Sightreading Challenge, No. 115
18. Page 24, EE Quiz, No. 120
19. Page 25, EE Quiz, No. 126
20. Page 27, EE Quiz, No. 133
21. Page 30, Natural Minor Scale, No. 144
22. Page 30, Harmonic Minor Scale, No. 146
23. Page 30, Pomp and Circumstance, No. 148
24. Page 31, Performance Spotlight
25. Page 32, Performance Spotlight
26. Page 33, Performance Spotlight
27. Page 38–39, Individual Study
28. Page 40, Performance Spotlight

MUSIC — AN ESSENTIAL ELEMENT OF LIFE

FINGERING CHART

Instrument Care Reminders

Before putting your instrument back in its case after playing, do the following:

- Use the water key to empty water from the instrument. Blow air through it.
- Remove the mouthpiece. Once a week, wash the mouthpiece with warm tap water. Dry thoroughly.
- Wipe off the instrument with a clean soft cloth. Return the instrument to its case.

Baritone valves occasionally need oiling. To oil your baritone valves:

- Unscrew the valve at the top of the casing.
- Lift the valve half-way out of the casing.
- Apply a few drops of special brass valve oil to the exposed valve.
- Carefully return the valve to its casing. When properly inserted, the top of the valve should easily screw back into place.

Be sure to grease the slides regularly. Your director will recommend special slide grease and valve oil, and will help you apply them when necessary.

CAUTION: If a slide, a valve or your mouthpiece becomes stuck, ask for help from your band director or music dealer. Special tools should be used to prevent damage to your instrument.

○ = Open
● = Pressed down

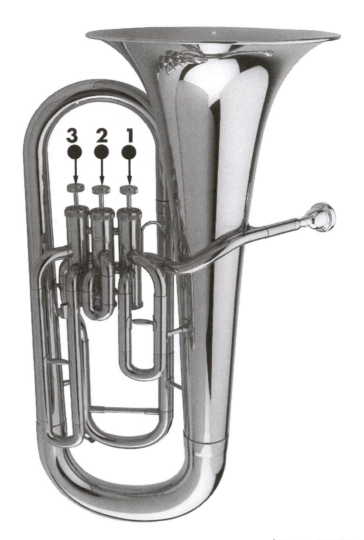

Instrument courtesy of Yamaha Corporation of America, Band and Orchestral Division

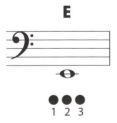

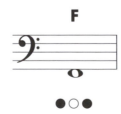

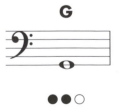

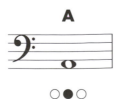

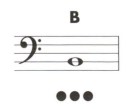

FINGERING CHART

C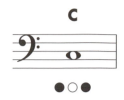
●○●

C♯ D♭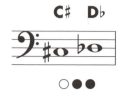
○●●

D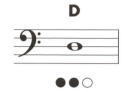
●●○

D♯ E♭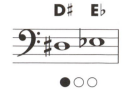
●○○

E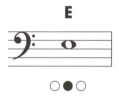
○●○

F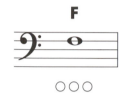
○○○

F♯ G♭
○●●

G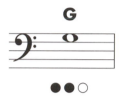
●●○

G♯ A♭
●○○

A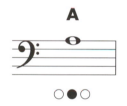
○●○

A♯ B♭
○○○

B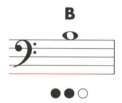
●●○

C
●○○

C♯ D♭
○●○

D
○○○

D♯ E♭
●○○

E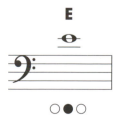
○●●

F
○○○

F♯ G♭
○●●

EFERENCE INDEX